CW01309865

The Changing of the Ways – Part Two 3
   INTRODUCTION 4
   THE GIG 5
   BENEATH YOUR COVID MASK 6
   EARS 7
   POST BREXIT - THIS GREEN AND PLEASANT LAND 8
   PIGGY BANK 10
   DEATH 11
   IN MEMORIAM - TINA MODOTTI Actress, Photographer and Spy 12
   COVENTRY 13
   THE SUNNY SWIMMING POOLS 14
   NOTHING EXISTS 15
   OF BEETLES; BOOTS AND BEER 16
   TIME 17
   TO WIN THE RACE 18
   COVID 19 19
   JANUARY 2021 20
   THE OLD POLE 21
   IF I COULD SEE ME 22
   LABOURS OF LOVE 24
   ALMS FOR THE POOR 25
   EXIT 26
   INDIGESTION 27
   FIRST OF JANUARY 28
   LIGHT 29
   OLYMPUS 30
   A POET'S THOUGHTS 31
   OLD GREY LANDROVER 32
   THE SOUL IS AS DEEP 33
   SONG FOR A SIX STRINGED LADY 34
   IN GERMANY, NOT LONG AGO 35
   EXILES IN PARIS, CIRCA 1920 36
   DREAM OF MY LIFE 38

THE WORLD OF MY HEROES	39
THE POEM	40
THE SCREEN	41
HOW MARVELLOUS THE MOVIES	42
A TOUNGE IN CHEEK ANSWER	44
IN THE MIDST OF A LOCKDOWN	46
THE VISION - a Limerick	47
THE PLEASURES OF DRIVING	48
PERFECTION	49
NOBLE WOOD	50
THE FASHION IS FOR PASSION	51
IN MEMORY OF SON HOUSE	52
MASOCHIST BLUES	53
TRUCKSTOP	54
BACK COMES THE NIGHT	56
FAT CHANCE	57
NOTHING SUCCEEDS LIKE SUCCESS	58
AMSTERDAM I	60
AMSTERDAM II	62
TONIGHT I AM JESUS	63
SARDINIA	64
BEAUTY	65
TIGER MOTH	66
TIME MACHINE	67
THE TIME OF MAN	68
THE HOLY WAR	70
THE FRIDAY PRAYERS	71
I REMEMBER HIM	72
UKRAINE I	74
UKRAINE II	76
MEMORIES AND EPILOGUE	78

3

The Changing of the Ways – Part Two

INTRODUCTION

Having known John Kirkbride for almost half a century, I´m aware (with a tinge of jealousy I must admit) that he is one of the finest fingerpicking acoustic guitarists you will ever see, Anywhere.... I've seen him play in smoky little bars with just a couple of dozen people hanging on his words.

I've seen him play amazing delta blues with John Mayall. receive rapturous applause as opener for Jethro Tull, and I've seen him return to the stage at a biker festival After Lemmy and Motörhead to keep a couple of thousand Jack Daniels inspired bikers happy till after 5 a.m

What I didn't know is that he writes poetry, I should have known of course, after all most of his songs are poetry in themselves. Well, this collection is the clincher, it made me laugh and it also brought tears to my eyes but above all, it made me think.

This book is something you can put in your pocket and delve into in a quiet moment. You will find something new every time.

John Kirkbride truly understands the power of language and the beauty of words.

Richard Fürst
Málaga
March 2022

5

THE GIG

I'm not the one to drink alone
But sometimes it seems that you have no choice
I put my guitar back on its stand
And sip my scotch (it does wonders for the voice)
The audience is moving around
Perhaps too shy to come and have a chat
They get their drinks and sit down again
Clutching the glass till the beer goes flat

Then a couple comes and shyly says hello
They mention how they enjoyed a certain song
I say it's one of my favourites too
I recite the lyrics but somehow get them wrong
They don't appear to notice my slip-up
Well, they probably never took in the words
Interesting that, for most, melody is quickly registered
While lyrics are as if they've never been heard

The break is over; the next set
Is all untested songs and new
The lights are pitiless, make me sweat
Fix my eyes on that delightful girl's tattoo
Cradle guitar. beautiful box
Fingers running over strings
G, followed by A minor
Immediate response, she sings

The girl with the tattoo gives me a smile
I can see she's aware that I've been looking
Her face is pretty, so's her hair
I can dig the cowboy shirt that she's wearing
Magic guitar sings the blues
The set goes by, like in a blur
She stands up, walks over to me
She must have known that we were singing for her

BENEATH YOUR COVID MASK

Your eyes are looking at me
And I'm aware of your voice
I hear your words
But words have nuances
Which I cannot decode
Beneath your Covid mask

You words have somehow
Sacrificed their meaning
With an immense loss of communication
The subtlety of expression
Grimace, smile or frown

Even the pursing of lips adds meaning
To verbal thoughts, but now
Your humanity has been taken
And rendered robotically indiscernible
I have lately become aware
That a word or phrase
Contains elusive import
That is lost
When I cannot see faces

Now I can almost imagine
What it must be like
For half of the population
Of Iran

EARS

There was surely a time
When mankind obtained only benefits and pleasure
From its ears
But I seem to be frequently involved in a situation
Of having to abuse them by having to lend them
To drunken monologues
Induced by whisky, cigarettes, drunken company
And beers

When youth driven cars cruise by open windowed
Emitting overpoweringly monologic bass
It's what is called rap (omitting the C)
I sometimes wish my ears
Were equipped with volume controls
So I could ignorantly and blissfully catnap

When I was a youth
Most of the people of my age
Had longish hair to camouflage the sight
Of these silhouette intruding protrusions, which
Reactivated by revellers at closing time
Forced me to lie awake at night

But my belief remains unaltered - that ears
Beside supporting both your sunglasses and your Covid mask
Have still more values for mankind
For example, listening to the silence of the stars moving
Across the sky while lying on the beach at night
Is a symphony that can always spellbind

8

POST BREXIT - THIS GREEN AND PLEASANT LAND

I will take the overheated handle
Of the overfull teapot
With dignity, despite the discomfort
After all, afternoon tea
Is a hallowed and dignified custom
To be preserved
For the sake of our national identity

I know that you're unconcerned about national identity
Or dignity, and that you penetrated this thin veneer
Of my armour years ago, as a small child
And I can live with the amusement in your eyes
We can be proud of our generations
Both you and I
You in your jeans and sweat shirt
Your confidence and worldliness
Me? I'll stick with my old but precious tweed jacket
As long as it protects my old but precious convictions

Your 're at home on - what are they called? Google, twitter?
While I'm still trying to fathom this new-fangled
mobile telephone you gave me. Still , it stops me grumbling
about the Austin Mini now being in German hands

9

I'm sorry I didn't enjoy the chinese takeaway
You brought with you last night
It somehow doesn't compare with steak and kidney pie and chips
With bread and butter
I know you're still amused
My identity, my national identity, this dignity
May well be held upright with the aid of this walking stick

But I have it, and have earned it
Protecting us from them
I'm sorry that we don't see everything eye to eye
But my generation has saved this green and pleasant land
Once again
For you

For us

Not them

PIGGY BANK

You're quite right
A piggy bank is the only safe deposit
for my money
I will invest in a bacon factory immediately

DEATH

Death is inevitable
Death is certain
So it's waste of what's left
Of your precious time
Sitting in windowless waiting rooms
With other silent suffering self-absorbed citizens
Trying to ward it off

At least the orchestra on the Titanic
Played
And were resigned
To their fate

IN MEMORIAM - TINA MODOTTI Actress, Photographer and Spy

I saw her in a photograph, which made her look so cold
And though I didn't know her story, her eyes seemed very old
I felt she'd seen the glow of dawn, and then again the blackest night
There was something hidden there, in a face so full of care
In a fading twilight

Indoctrinated with some truth, but she surely knew it was a lie
No longer burdened with her youth she knew that she could only try
to right the wreckage of her life which burning love had torn apart
In everything she tried to do, each photograph, each something new
she was the prisoner of her heart

She followed love from land to land, from the west to the east
At a time when this frail world had been invaded by the beast
I read the book between the lines, I know that love had made her strong
and even when love went astray she lived to love another day
She could survive when love went wrong

Accused of something she'd not done, but too tired to deny
She returned to her nest, but the nest had grown dry
And the heart she had offered to each love, to each new day
One day suddenly stood still , like the sails of a mill
when the wind fades away

The times she had known, the lips she had kissed
were suddenly gone, simply did not exist
The pain she had suffered, the life she had seen
Were removed from this earth, like a stillborn birth
As if it never had been

COVENTRY

It was more than just surprise
It was a revelation

A stone tablet set into the wall
of the hospital corridor

in Dresden

read:

We beg forgiveness from the
citizens and city of Coventry
for the loss of life and the
destruction which took place
due to the bombing on

14th November 1940

The tablet pleased me.
It was a noble gesture

Among my acquaintances in Germany
the war was seldom, if ever, talked about,
which is understandable.

But I do admit to an element of doubt
as to whether the people who took the
trouble to read the tablet even knew
in which country Coventry was situated

and if it was the German Luftwaffe
which bombed it

14

THE SUNNY SWIMMING POOLS

The sunny swimming pools
of the world
will forget my body
But remember yours
I could easily disregard
their disdainful glances
at my pallid body
If you could remember it
With some affection
I remember your body
With the wonder
of the old time explorer
as you lay naked on the rug
before the fire
The leaping flames gave
your satin skin
that quality of mystery
which urged my questing mouth
to the oldest secrets of the world

NOTHING EXISTS

Nothing exists
Save the curve of your mouth
The sun, the sky, the sea and the people
Have all faded into nothingness
I never know that lips could say so much
Without sound
Obscenely reddened against the whiteness
Of your teeth
Without speaking
They do not smile
They do not show distaste .
They observe
They look
They stare
They move
fluently
They twist, they writhe
And still they stare
come closer
grow larger
surround
and engulf me
Now they are laughing
I am lost

OF BEETLES; BOOTS AND BEER

"Mister, please don't step on me"
The tiny beetle cried
'I've got to cross six paving stones
before there's a place to hide
I 've a wife and sixteen kids to feed
not twenty feet from here
I don't want to be flattened by your bloody great boot
and leave me just a smear"

Resigned, he watched the cloud descend
to end his little life
Wondering who would notice
and who would tell his wife
But it was only due to the seventh pint
and pressure on the bladder
that the would-be killer abruptly turned
or this tale would be much sadder

The giant ship descending, swerved
to face a nearby tree
To leave our beetle pale and shocked
as if some god had heard his plea
It's recorded that he lived to tell
this story to his wife
The only time that seven pints
have saved a beetle's life

TIME

If time approaches on the street
I will not run, I will not cheat
I will not turn, hide my face
Nor any steps retrace
I'll boldly face him, unafraid
The life is done, the mad crusade
I'll need no-one to offer aid
I'll take my fate with grace

If time should take me by the hand
Why brace myself for one last stand
He knows I've made my last goodbye
And will not beg for reprieve
I will not tremble, will not shake
At any motion he may make
Or clasp the soul that he must take
When time has come to leave

You'll feel me smile at your concern
From life and death we all must learn
So dance and celebrate for me
And let your soul be free
The carousel slows, the race is run
The music fades, what's done is done
I shed no tears, I've had my fun
I leave by high decree

I charge you with my last request
Take accoutrements, the worthless rest
They will not help me pass some test
I leave with which I came
I'll accept the judgement, come what may
Without resistance, I will obey
I feel sorrow for your sad dismay
At the passing of my flame

TO WIN THE RACE

The knowledge that
at the age of seventy-five
many of my old acquaintances and friends
have passed away
fills me with a certain sadness
and perhaps a sense of loneliness
that moments shared and remembered
by both of us and found amusing
are now remembered only by one
and laughing alone
is more difficult

I have heard
that there are those of my generation
who entertain ambitions to outlive
all of their old chums
To win the race, so to speak
But I can't, for the life of me
see the reason why it's so impressive
to stand alone on top of the mountain
sensing the emptiness of the void below
hearing the icy wind laughing
But no cheering throng

COVID 19

Our enemy, the virus

does not love
does not hate
has no evil thoughts

unlike humanity

it has no thoughts
no feelings
no emotions

it just is

and does what viruses do

replicate where possible
mutate where possible to

ensure the survival of the species

I seem to remember

that a certain Charles Darwin
wrote about this

and as we are now battling and experiencing
the proof of his theory

certain areas of the United States
should finally bow before the once,
but no longer, revolutionary theories
of a thinking man and scientist

20

JANUARY 2021

We've had no snow for some years now
At least, not like it was
when I was a lad
But in the midst of a dreary lockdown
interrupted only by news of another crisis
somewhere in the world
Here it is again

Snow is back!
Amazing!
In the midst of global warming
I hear that Madrid is suffering with minus 20c
while my brother, living in Norway
Is jogging in a mere minus 2c

It's a funny old world
But at least it's not boring
Correction; lockdown is boring
Soul destroying
for those too restless to read or write
or those (like me) incapable of
redecorating the living room
or something

But just imagine
In six months
thirty degrees in Andalusian
We've all been vaccinated
The kids are back in school
A Covid free future stretches before us

And suddenly everyone forgets

Covid 19

and global warming

THE OLD POLE

The old Pole
is not afraid that the noise
of his boots on the cobblestones
will wake his enemies

He has no more enemies

He is ninety-one years old
He has many memories
To think about
He is quite correct
He was a fisherman

His enemies and his comrades
of youth have long since passed away

He is not concerned with the latest
demands and proposals of the
government
He has outlived
the latest proposals

The science of vodka production
is of no concern to him
He knows only that it helps

He is not preoccupied with death
He is not tortured by poetry
He does not tear his flesh at the
sight of a female thigh
He sits outside when the sun is warm
He sits inside when it rains
He is a sensible man

IF I COULD SEE ME

If I could see me through your eyes
What would I think of me
Would I see the man I think I am
of what I try to be

Would I feel the taste inside my mouth
and the pain between my eyes
and the torment felt in wrestling words
while trying to be wise

If I could see me through your eyes
would I shudder at my taste
Pants held up with a scuffed old belt
Round a non-existent waist

A bearded, boozy, balding bum
with a guitar in his hand
Singing songs of love and hate
no-one can understand

If I could see me through your eyes
would I buy myself a drink
In the hope I'd splash some sense inside
and make me start to think

Maybe get a haircut, buy a suit
a nice white shirt and tie
and sell my soul for a fat bankroll
until the day I die

23

If I could see me through your eyes
would I sense the deja vu
Would it bring back someone I had known
back in nineteen sixty two
Would I see the sprightly lanky youth

with a skin that's now too wide
And divine the values he had held
still buried deep inside
If I could see me through your eyes
would I try to modify

the way I drink your femaleness
with a twinkle in my eye
Would I put my arms around me
and lead me to the bar
and say, I love me as I am
Yes, just the way you are

LABOURS OF LOVE

Shakespeare would have known what to say about this
A smile is a smile and a kiss is a kiss
Hearts can be broken a love to create
Heads can be broken when they retaliate

Human nature is hard to define
Love walks side by side but it will not stand in line
It sometimes goes crazy and the paths deviate
What at daybreak was kisses in the evening is hate

At least it's not tedious, that's all I can say
I've been hearing the screams as I go on my way
Let that be a lesson, if you value your skin
Don't look in their eyes and let the heartbreak begin

An exquisite torture sent down from above
A debt to be paid for the pleasure of love
Sustenance for Hollywood and books by those females
Whose writing resemble some kid's fairy tales

Nero bathed blissfully in the kisses of his boys
They were innocent puppets, sure all lovers are toys
But love's sweetest moments can be the pretext for assault
Let your escape route be planned, even if it's not your fault

ALMS FOR THE POOR

ALMS for the poor
ALMS for the poor
A familiar song that is heard no more

The church took God
The church took God
But they have no mercy on this poor sod

Show him to the court
Lock him in jail
Lucky that he can't afford no bail
Dress him in chains
Take him away
Give him to the citizens and let them play

Give him bread and water
Turn off the heat
Our profits are eaten if we give him meat

He has earned no rights
Let him die
There's no-one in this song to cry

The grass is green
But the grave is cold
God had no mercy on his soul

EXIT

I blocked off my exit to the world

When I touched love

Everybody needs love

Everybody needs an exit

I suppose the decision is
Which do I need most

INDIGESTION

If your patient whistling
is in tune with the sounds of your indigestion
and your headache provides an accompanying
rhythmic percussion
If you can believe that the discomfort
does not exist
If you can believe in God the father
The brotherhood of man
and the neighbourhood of the Dog and Partridge

That the present discomfort in America
cannot be compared to yours
If you have no feelings towards this president
not only because you are not American
but also because you can ignore the pain
of others

Then you may find that some of this poetry
may help you
Not, I hastily add, that I ignore America completely

or this president but I believe in the important things of life

Like music for example

And my indigestion knows several interesting tunes
which I am happy to pass on

FIRST OF JANUARY

Once again the first of January dawns
with its usual wintry and miserable grimace

Only this year it is different

I can afford to offer an unseen smile
in return, beneath my covid mask

I have carried nothing over
from the old year

Not even one lonely and vulnerable

Resolution

LIGHT

I used to allow no light
to enter my room
when I pretended my body
was somebody else

I used to study the newspapers
carefully
Hoping some other sinner would be
caught

And condemned

Not me

but also to know that I was not so alone

with my sin

But so far the threatened finger of God
has not condemned me

Maybe He has become more tolerant

OLYMPUS

Was it last night I dreamed I was
washed clean be the rain and
for a time became a man
Not as you know him
but something more godlike

Cast from Olympus for some trivial sin
but nevertheless all-seeing, all discerning
Unwilling amidst filth and corruption
but disinclined to change it

observing good and evil, noble and demonic
But averse to forming an opinion
Shake hands with Hitler
Impress him with the nonchalance of gods

But, as Titus became unconvinced of the
the existence of Gormenghast
becoming unsure of that of Olympus
Ah, these square german words

leave no gaps when fitted together
No way of escape
Still, does it matter?
Brothers, let me tell you right now
We don't care to fight any more, us gods
Future legends told us we would lose
and, no longer captivated with the grammar of warriors
I am happy to change
Al though the battle map looks so artistic
with all those coloured pins
But don't try to tell me it means something
If it means something

it is lost forever
And for an instant
I sense the truth
Then Olympus is forgotten
Forever

A POET'S THOUGHTS

A poet's thoughts may wander far
For words that lend description
To the contents of a mini-bar
In amorous depiction
He'll bend each word to suit his needs
He'll cut and modify
And when the rhyme he seeks succeeds
He'll drain the bottle dry

Every drop poured down his throat
The poet will inspire
And he'll try to decipher what he wrote
as the mini-bar gets drier
At three o'clock his weary pen
Falls from his lifeless fingers
As the sherry sweet aroma of
Glendronach subtly lingers

OLD GREY LANDROVER

Old grey Land Rover
I would choose rather to be carried
on your unsophisticated
and somewhat uncomfortable back

than that of your pampered and privileged sisters
Mercedes and Co
Whose glassy eyed stares
and carefully cultivated characters

somehow leave my desires unawakened
Playmates' of the upper class
They would never respond to me with a gentle purr
If they were aware of my empty pockets

Old military companion
I've relished your bumpy rumble
over deserts and dirt tracks
Highways and holiday resorts

You and I have parked at the barracks and beaches
of the world
And we can still hold our heads high
amongst the snobbiest of the higher social status
and these modern four wheel drive nonentities

The chauffeur of princes and generals you have been
You honourable old devil
And today you honour me with your presence once again

To have one more dance together

THE SOUL IS AS DEEP

The soul is as deep as the river that flows
Cradled in valleys which only it knows
Committed and constant it flows to the sea
Of others in limbo who wait patiently

To take place in the hearts of a new generation
To join once again in that constant creation
Yet, knowing their fate, that when they are needed
Compassionate virtues will seldom be heeded

These souls are not silent, they have much to relate
Of love and of passion, of kindness and hate
Of mankind's impatience, too hurried to learn
These things are considered while waiting their turn

To embark on this journey, for good or for ill
Charged with this mission, life to instill.
Serene, though yet conscious of what may be their fate
If the essence they bear is too little, too late

SONG FOR A SIX STRINGED LADY

Well the jug is nearly empty and the fire's burning low
Worn my boots so long that I can't feel my toes
And my guitar strings are singing songs of lonesome and of love
She's shared adventures with me, and it shows

She ain't lost her magic with the passing of the years
She can turn a simple rhyme into a song
She can make a strong man open up and show the world his fears
She can make a wounded soul once more be strong

She can help a man remember; she can help a man forget
Though she doesn't look like much, just old and worn
But I've held her body closely every night since we first met
She sounds sweeter now than the day that she was born

She knows all the answers that the world has yet to learn
And she tells them in a soft and gentle way
She's just too young to threaten but too old to show concern
But she'll lay on you the things she has to say

The ghosts of lonely struggles are reflected in her song
In mighty storms and lonely seagull's cries
And the blaze of a million campfires take their place where she belongs
Glowing in the distance of your eyes

Sometimes she makes me laugh and then again, she makes me cry
Sometimes she'll raise the snow and wind and rain
And I know that I will need her until the day I die
Like a self-inflicted torture without pain

And now she's quietly sleeping, lying gentle on the ground
And you wonder how she ever made it seem
Like your soul was overflowing with the silver of her sound
Like a long-lost friend or a long-forgotten dream

IN GERMANY, NOT LONG AGO

In Germany, long ago
I met a boy who didn't know
the lessons learned from history
or else his eyes just could'nt see

or perhaps because he had no need
of membership in some old creed
to tell him what he should believe
what message should his soul receive

so living life as it appeared
his happiness somehow endeared
him to a lovely girl of darker skin
who, trying to convince her kin
that love itself is colour blind
can touch the hearts of all mankind
in the name of Islam she was slain
to wipe away the accursed stain

bestowed upon the family
who knew it not, but are doomed to be
bit players in a tragic tale
where gods and kings and bigots fail

to seek the truth although it's plain
that we one day shall once again
return in mind from whence we came
acknowledging our bitter shame

accepting that idols gods and nation state
can sow the seeds of bitter hate
invoke the names of them in vain
for others will inflict more pain

like those whose hearts with hate were filled
and mindlessly their sister killed
in Germany not long ago
I just thought you ought to know

EXILES IN PARIS, CIRCA 1920

City of light, queen of the night
I guess you've seen it all
Saints and sinners, people like us
Who heeded to your call

Laughing, drinking, dancing, thinking
In this exile, self imposed
You gave us no glance, you had no need to care
Your eyes were tightly closed

Street lights cast shadows as we strolled through your streets
Rejoicing in the magic of your summer night
Pretending we'd found freedom and other conceits
Intemperate shadows in the pale and ghostly light

The forcefulness of passions that erupted
When and love met in a blur
Paris, if I could cry for a city
I would cry for the loss of what you were

Though comrades, we knew how to disagree
But by our culture bound together
A fear of exile during exile was
An invisible, communal tether

If other doors were closed to us
We could prowl the streets at night
Divorced from your reality, Paris
Reality was shielded from our sight

We wandered through the alleys, the back streets and the bars
Convinced that youth was timeless, and for ever
Absolved of responsibilities, the moment was the thing!
I remember how we thought we so clever

Now the wonder we once knew has turned to ashes

Your gaily laughing crowds are deaf and dumb
Paris, if I could cry for a city
I would cry to see the thing you have become

Paris, you seduced us then
Like nothing in our lives has since achieved
We always thought, with the battle lost
Our garrison could always be relieved
We screamed for love, you offered us pain
And we never noticed that you didn't even care
We never realised that you'd seen it all before
And had no need to offer us a prayer

DREAM OF MY LIFE

Dream of my life, through the worst of my days
You have stayed by my side, never lavish with praise
I have followed the path of your musical voice
You have shown me the way and have left me the choice
I can sense that you are so much stronger than me
Though possessing my thoughts, you still let me be free
Within the alliance of music and rhyme
An honour worthy of devoting a lifetime

The virtues of heroes, the honour of thieves
Mean nothing to someone who merely believes
That they only exist in the pages of prose
From those writers of fiction who have no need to compose

It is good, or is evil, curiosity stilled
The need to build higher is broken and killed
Then the battle is over, or not yet begun
Then how can they know if they've lost or have won

Dream of my life, at the dawn of new years
Your silent seclusion awakens the fears
That we never shall meet and rejoice in the end
That the journey was made without meeting a friend
Have you been sacrificed for the sake of a scheme
To clear from obstruction the place of my dream
Should I discard you now in the hope that there'll be
An illusion of fulfilment waiting for me

Dream of my life, should we live by the rules
Of the world we inhabit, and suffer the fools
Who believe that the fires of evil are held
From the forests of goodness which cannot be felled

By musical waters bequeathed to all men
As a promise that slaughter will not happen again
Or to follow your voice in the search for the truth
That you promised to me in the glory of youth

THE WORLD OF MY HEROES

Sometimes I can close my eyes
And be awakened to cool memories of country lanes
Shadowy, even furtive
The world of my heroes
Before the passage of time
decided I should become a man

A wide world it was, brimming with miraculous promise
Where crab apples served as hand grenades
Sticks became deadly weapons
when loaded
And it was no great surprise
to encounter the idols of W.E. Johns or Defoe
face to face
This mysterious world of my heroes

In this heroic world
it was permissible to walk backwards if so desired
Or drag toes through the damp warmth of autumn leaves
When bruised knees were familiar objects
Love was for sissies
and washing was a ritual to be avoided
whenever possible
And my education was of interest
only to adults

I give thanks for those cool memories
before time decided
I should be a man

THE POEM

All the rivers we crossed
In the search for improvement
All the bridges we burned
all the love that has died
Like a pale winter scene
with no life and no movement
as we seek inspiration
That words clarify

Then the warm golden hope
of the dawn's blue horizon
Then a cloud drifts across
and the words start to fail
A poem is truth but you feel
that it's lies and
only honesty can help you when
relating your tale

The beauty of language
creating a picture
of meanings and legends
and people we've known
Remembered in verse
without stretch without stricture
Just honest and simple
as if embedded in stone

So this is the pain
in the heart of the poet
The rhythm of language
The joy of the word
To write it in colours
so the plain man will love it
So truthful and candid
and fit to be heard

41

THE SCREEN

The screen will never communicate the truth
It's usually an exaggerated vision of youth
only possible because of human impressionability
which doesn't add to the screenplay's reliability
It's entertaining if you have no need to think
Eat your popcorn, settle down, have a drink
Don't ever think that you could try to make correction
It's been cut and spliced to run in one direction

I'm not saying that it tells exactly lies
This Technicolor screenplay paradise
and if the movie you are watching is too boring
There's a million more that you could be exploring
It's nail-biting to see the lover shoot his rival
It's a Hollywood confirmation of love's survival
And so the budding of this now conflict free romance
Might send the girl beside you into a trance

The movie's over and you're outside on the street
But it can feel like an admission of defeat
The people walking by you seem so small
The ones back on the screen seemed ten feet tall
The women really knew how to dress
While the one standing beside you is a mess
Makes you think - maybe real life isn't that good
Why ain't it just a little more like Hollywood

HOW MARVELLOUS THE MOVIES

How marvellous the movies when I was a kid
Like going on a wondrous journey
The hero revealing
the dirtiest dealings
of the crooked District Attorney
It always felt right in its plain black and white
The scenes so weird and mysterious
Bogart in a trench coat
With Lauren Bacall
They weren't acting - it was real and they were serious

Wednesdays, I remember, was half price for kids
Including popcorn for seven and six
Smuggle in your fags
(it was dark in the stalls)
Everybody smoked in the flicks
Cagney was tough and we couldn't get enough
of his grin and American drawl
He seemed a big man
to our eyes on the screen
I was surprised that he was really quite small

When the hero lit up we all lit up as well

You could hardly see the screen for the haze
But the tough guy expressions
we were practising like mad
were shielded from everyone's gaze
I got my first kiss at the back of the stalls
I remember her name - it was Judy
I would have tried more
But I hadn't the balls
I reckon that's why she turned moody

The Sunday matinees with Chaplin and Keaton

43

We were hysterical the whole way through
We were raising the laughs with the hilarious gaffes
of the Keystone Cops who hadn't a clue
Laurel and Hardy always went down well
One being of our island race
On the big silver screen!
And he seldom was seen
As the one with the pie in his face

How marvellous the movies when I was a kid
I don't go there much any more
The real stars are gone

they've mostly passed on
and dinos are a bloody great bore
Don't even watch telly - well that's even worse
Prefer to settle down with a good book
Some writer like Simenon and those of his ilk
Who can create a believable crook

44

A TOUNGE IN CHEEK ANSWER.....

A tongue in cheek answer to a tongue in cheek question from a charming Japanese lady of my acquaintance:

Dear Mayuko,

The question of why the human male generally requires more than one sexual partner when he has only been kitted out with one penis is an interesting one and deserves a detailed answer. It is not merely "proving himself" by simply boosting his ego. It is more of a physical necessity, but it also has an enormous social relevance which can create serious misunderstandings between partners. These can perhaps be cleared up with a bit of tolerance and information.

The fact that the male possesses one penis (colloquially "dick") but two testicles (col. "bollocks") is even today not fully explained, but the symbiotic function between the three is highly relevant to answering the question. The bollocks are being continuously replenished with sperm, and in the case of non-ejaculation pressure inside them naturally increases, causing the owner of the said bollock to seek relief. The bollocks hang helplessly in their little sack (scrotum) so it falls to the dick to effect the necessary release. Dick sends a message to the brain, (such as it is), saying n cunt, or equivalent needed, pronto" This SMS is the instigator of many a chatting up at sleazy hotel bars over Jacky and Cokes and gins and tonics, accompanied by half-smoked cigarettes, lit with a slightly shaking hand. The final "over the top" in this pseudo-social operation falls to dick. He is forced to stand to attention like a member of the household cavalry whilst performing an arduous drilling job which would put a Welsh miner to shame, before being forced, finally, to throw up before collapsing, exhausted.

Evolution, which ensures the survival of the more successful developments in nature, has not shortened the lengthy arms which we inherited from our primate forebears, by very much. For this we can be grateful . It enables the human male, by practically strangling dick, to relieve the pressure without seeking relief at hotel bars.

45

Females execute something generally along the same lines when necessary, but with an absence of the strangulation hold. This solo operation, however, is historically disapproved of in human society. The human being is a social animal . Solo is out. This has given rise to legends of the growth of hair on the palms of the hands, not to mention palsy, among other terrifying things.

The female, though vaguely interested in copulation, does not suffer from the pressure which torments the male. She is genetically equipped with a number of ready and convenient excuses to avoid her fundamental duty, and these are familiar to males: "I've got a splitting headache", "my period has just started", "I haven't finished cleaning yet! and, to top it all , "l've got a yeast infection down there". She conveniently forgets that she is fully equipped with a set of various orifices, any of which would suffice to relieve the pressure. Copulation, when it does take place, can generally be conducted within a span of time to suit her, even as little as thirty seconds, which is often the case.

Prudishness, a trait which became ridiculously prevalent in Victorian times, has survived, most notably in the USA. It is not a natural peculiarity of the human. The great apes do not suffer from it, and neither, apparently, did our human ancestors. Historical documents often describe sexual orgies, sometimes surrounded by interested and cheering onlookers offering advice and occasionally joining in.

And in that particular scenario, a dick or two extra can be a useful bonus

IN THE MIDST OF A LOCKDOWN

In the midst of a lockdown
It's hard to get your nose brown
But some politicians in London
Are doing just that.
They adore the Prime Minister
Whose motives are sinister
And treat him like Jesus
Instead of a twat

In spite of their posing
And all their brown nosing
Their days are all numbered
As they shortly will see
A number of these wankers
Should be sentenced to jankers
Where an enterprising jailor
Will just lose the key

Their ex-comrade in Washington
That clown and comedian
Had been fucking his nation
Like a maddened messiah
He transformed the white house
To a luxury shite house
For a narcissistic asshole
And professional liar

Their airs and their graces
And the grins on their faces
Will all fade away
Like the fabled Cheshire cat
They will take their immaturity
Into well-deserved obscurity
Like a shite-stained impurity
And that will be that

THE VISION - a Limerick

Last night in my dreams, I had a vision
Which led to a spontaneous decision
It, was lovely, with brown hair
And it had nothing to wear
And it looked at me with noticeable derision

Well you cannot get hold of a dream
No matter how real it may seem
You can be sure that I tried
My dream to bestride
But no way could I close the division

I was aware of it starting to frown
My attempts made me look like a clown
So I felt I was free
To clutch that part of me
Which was generally left to hang down

The finale of this concise narration
Was a satisfying mutual masturbation
And after the event
We both came and she went
Leaving me liberated from my frustration

THE PLEASURES OF DRIVING

The pleasures of driving
Lie not in arriving
but in the exquisite torment
of a sweet traffic jam
This impromptu meeting
with comfortable seating
is for wearied commuters
a respite in programme

But the intensity of the pleasure
at the resulting leisure
may quickly disperse
if you're going nowhere
Things can also get sadder
with pressure on the bladder
and a pee would expose you
to that inquisitive stare

Road works may trouble you
in your high-powered BMW
But you can be revenged
in the fullness of time
by replacing that minister
with another, less sinister
and improved infrastructure
Not this pantomime

PERFECTION

After finishing toenails, fingernails, eyebrows
Flossing teeth and snipping hair
Searching through mounds of discarded clothes
Undecided what to wear
Carefully applying the various potions
To imaginary imperfections of her skin
The lassie slowly transforms herself
To a vision which many men would care to win

A daub of perfume here and there
Feminine perfection
Surveying the mirror, sees one thing
For which she has no affection
North of thighs, it meets her eyes
No way to get it styled
The hair grows thickly, bestial relic
Uncombed and happily wild

Men may be hirsute, women - never
She has thoroughly shaved each armpit
But her vision of perfection is outraged
By this unlovely, untameable fleapit
She sits herself before the mirror
Parts her thighs and wields the blade
A dedicated female artist
Get it off - get it flayed

She knows it won't be easy
To reach every little bit
The folds are complicated
And be careful of the clit
But the job is finally finished
And she can smile down at her front
At that which once was pussy
Is a desolate, naked, cunt

NOBLE WOOD

You're leaning up against the wall
My Japanese guitar
and I look at you, contemplating
Just how beautiful you are

You could outshine any beauty queen
with the perfection of your line
And in contrast to the human voice
your singing is divine

Your harmonies hypnotic
Even dissonance exotic
The blues in you erotic
The perfect concubine

Chain saws felled that noble tree
where there your mother stood
But they never got to kill your soul
Child of noble wood

I want to take you in my arms
stroke your silver strings
Rousing you from your musical dreams
to give my lost soul wings

THE FASHION IS FOR PASSION

The fashion is for passion
Of the public viewing kind
Not just a sordid little blowjob
Beneath the bedclothes of your mind
The things we never talked about
by unspoken decree
Are now all on the internet
For all the world to see

You could say that it's a bit tasteless
to reveal our most private lives
Which are mostly dull and graceless
But the prying eye survives
I can still remember "Brave New World"
I read it as a kid
Where the hero, camera conscious, tried
to keep his secrets hid:

Now it's easy to be famous
For a fleeting tick of time
See the gormless ignoramus
With his fatuous pantomime
Even normal TV shows
Today are fairly lousy
But all this muck you are invited to look
at, does nothing but make me drows

IN MEMORY OF SON HOUSE

The blues they was a-turning
Like a wheel within a wheel
Son House his head was churning
Over gleaming cold cold steel
And the cold steel she was singing
Hey Son, you and me's the blues.
You're the one who really knows how
Knows how to light my fuse

Son's hands were moving gracefully
And he held cold steel real tight
And her body it was blinding
As it shimmered in the light
Son House was coming home now
Yeas, he started coming down
From serving his soul to the working people
In the shabby part of town

He moaned and he hollered
He was lost inside his pain
And cold steel she was whining
As the blues made her insane
Yeah, cold steel was the bullet
And Son he was the gun
And magic of his memory
Will linger on and on

The memory he left us
Is the highest point of art
The collective blues emotion
Of which Son was a massive part
The poetry of emotion
Yes the poetry of pain
Was an accident of history
And will never come again

MASOCHIST BLUES

Well your arms are brawny - like a percussionist
You got the craziest mouth - that I've ever kissed
our beamis broad - and your shoulders too
And I can't explain - why I'm in love with you

You can pick me up - using just one arm
And your tone of voice - is devoid of charm
When you need some loving - it's like a royal command
You leave me dead and gone - you're like a firebrand

If you're a terrorist - then I'm a masochist
Just picking up -on what you think I've missed
You can leave me for dead -beside the bed
But at least I know where I've been

Your arms are mighty - like a blacksmith's vice
But I ain't complaining - I think that's nice
And your treasure chest - can cut out sound
I take a real deep breath - and go underground

Your hair is short - just like barbed wire
And the way you walk - says gun for hire
You drink my scotch - neat and in doubles
And you lie on the bed - like a mountain of troubles

You can call it passion - but it's more like rage
And when it comes to fashion - you don't act your age.
My future looks bleak - my well-being too
So I can't explain - why I'm in love with you

54

TRUCKSTOP

It was just a regular truck stop on the interstate just north of Nashville. Nothing special. A bit run down but the neon lights were all up and flashing as I parked.
I wasn't hungry but I just needed a break.
There were four or five trucks parked and a couple of cars.
Obviously not rush hour so it wouldn't be crowded.

I went in. Nine Formica covered tables, four of which were occupied. Three with what were obviously truckers, two of whom were eating steak and eggs, and in the corner a coloured family, mom and dad and two sweet kids about seven or eight, the pretty little girl with pigtails and the little boy wearing a clean and often washed New York
Yankees T-shirt.

The waitress, a skinny peroxide blonde wearing ultra tight jeans and slight food stained blouse, was deep in conversation with the barman at the counter and appeared not to notice the customers waiting to order. We just sat there. Several minutes passed. The door opened and four men entered. Two sat down together and the others took seats at . separate tables. The waitress suddenly woke up to the realization that there were customers, and pulled out a pencil and jotter started walking around the tables taking orders.

The colored family were ignored.

I ordered a coke. The waitress was noisily chewing gum and had an accent radically different from that of New York, together with a voice which was harsh und whining. The door opened and another couple entered. They sat down and the waitress went over to them.

The coloured family, obviously waiting to order, appeared to be invisible.

55

My coke came. Beer for two of the tables and a coffee for the woman who had come in last. Two truckers were served with food. The waitress returned to the counter between every sortie to continue her interminable discussion with the barman.

The coloured kids, obviously hungry, were beginning to wriggle with impatience. I overheard the mother telling them to keep still and they'd be served shortly. The waitress noticed me again and came over with a pencil poised. "Maybe y'all ' d like something t'eat now?
"'Sure . Maybe you could deal with the family in the corner there first. They were here before me".
Her face, hard and pinched as it was, became even harder. "Listen mister, I do my job and I don't need no advice on how to go about it. Who d'y'all think y'are?"
I stood up. Plunked three dollars on the table. "Down south," I said. "But I didn't think I was that far south.
I left.
I hope she took the advice on how to do her job seriously.

BACK COMES THE NIGHT

We thought that hate was long behind us
Back comes the night
We'd thought an age of peace would find us
But back comes the night
We'd finally killed Mankind's obsession.
With ethnic cleansing, cold oppression
Racist rage and blind aggression
Back comes the night

How nonpartisan are you my friend
In this darkest night
Are you caught up in this heedless trend
In this darkest night
Religious shades of every hue
Though Muslim, Christian, Buddhist Jew
Are mostly folks like me and you
But back comes the night

The age of reason has departed
In this darkest night
And left our future still uncharted
In this darkest night
History, once again repeated
Indoctrination, so conceited
Hate filled rhetoric, greatly heated
Back comes the night

FAT CHANCE

There really is a fat chance
that I could learn to tap dance
Even standard dancing is beyond my ken
I'd never take the risk, no
while drinking in the disco
At the bar strictly tied to the world
of men

I'm doomed to stay a barfly
I wouldn't even care to try
to cut a dashing figure on the floor
I would hear for ever after
the ringing of the laughter
of the females and some other clowns
who scream for more

NOTHING SUCCEEDS LIKE SUCCESS

Nothing succeeds like success
But first drag yourself from the mess
The one you created by just being born
Relationships since have been tattered and torn
You're an object of amusement, an object to scorn
Humanity's clinging abscess
Some people are born to succeed
To have influence, fame and to lead
To sit on the throne at the top of the pile
To bequeath those beneath them a tolerant smile
 While you're at the bottom, a beast to revile
And society couldn't care less

They say that it's tough at the top
But I know it's tougher down here
Some days I just wish it would stop
And just sit around and drink beer
I know I was meant for great things
But the things that Mm best at ain't great
The thing that I'm best at just brings
Another cold stiff to cremate

Nothing succeeds like success
Brings girls to a state of undress
The ones you or night meet on a smart private jet
A very far cry from the scrubbers we get
Invite them for a drink and you'll end up in debt
And you won't even get her address
They say that it's tough at the top
 But I can't say that I quite agree

59

Orwell said that all men are equal
But most are more equal than me
I know I was meant to draw crowds
But when I do they just scream and throw stuff
I don't care much if they get loud

But it pisses me when they get rough
Nothing succeeds like success
An arduous and murky process
There's no hope at all for an utopian fairy tale
With no clothes and no car and no talent for sale
Make just one mistake and you'll end up in jail
And they'll be sure that they'll make you confess

AMSTERDAM I

I prefer to lean against the deck railing and watch the ducks in their aimless and endless journeys along the slimy waterways, perhaps meeting old friends for the first time since last summer saying hi may your feathers never grow less.
Jerry, who is taking a leak into the water remarks that there is too much traffic noise here to attempt to busk and why don't we look for a quieter place.

We seek, and in the Calverstraat sit on the steps of an imposing building between the pigeon droppings and ice-cream cartons. It's a bank. One of the financial centres of a financial nation and why shouldn't some of that finance come our way.
Unwrap the guitars, check for old bill out of the corners of our eyes and try a bit of fingerpicking, the old leather Spanish hat on the ground in front of us.

Amusing to see the affluent tourist and the skinny jeans clad junkie drop a coin in the hat while the well-dressed local suburbanites look away and stroll by. Fifteen minutes pass and we have a pretty large audience, and someone whispers cops, so we grab the hat and flee down a side street into a cafe where we order two beers.

Five minutes later the hippy looking guy who warned us walks in and asks us if we've got a place to stay this night and we say yeah, the Vondelpark and he says it's okay if we stay on his boat. Visions of comfort. It transpires, after a half hour walk, to be a broken-down old barge, leaks plugged with a variety of solutions, in the depths of which an emaciated and aromatic figure is enjoying the sleep of the innocent.

61

Kind hearted and unusual hospitality cemented with tea and smokes. Pleasant conversation. Swap adventures old and new, real and imaginary and we empty the hat to supply finances for the eats in the café down the road which becomes our sitting room for the evening, the owner looking on with some amazement at the appearance of glinting dutch coin.

To the supermarket for three bottles of wine. Anyone passing the boat that night must have his heart gladdened by the flickering candle lit sounds of laughter and conversation mingled with the gentler tones of guitar.
And to sleep, with peace in our hearts.

AMSTERDAM II

I can only force myself to be
a survivor
of the morning after

Leaving them all still sleeping
in their squalor
Sprawled - a hand here, a face there

Open mouthed

A multitude of snores of various disharmonious pitches which lazily
penetrate the early morning fog
of body odour

Up on deck a nebulous
chill of morning air
caresses my face

Usually I would perhaps think of coffee
as a useful agent of recovery
but all that now enters my mind is the tranquillity Peacefulness
strangely actually accentuated
by the early morning chirping
of the sparrows
and the gentle lapping of the watery gracht
beneath my feet

Chilly freshness
The morning sun, having no other movement to look at
Looks at me

I return his unblinking stare with defiance

A golden arc tinkling in the water below

TONIGHT I AM JESUS

Tonight I am Jesus
Suffering for my world
but knowing that I can love freely
and forgive all in my circle
save one

As you sit beside me and laugh
not only at my jokes
but his also
Your lips glistening with the wine
fermented with innocent devotion
I know in my heart of your betrayal to come
at the fleeting moment
 when we touch true perspective

Tonight I cannot long for you
Tonight you are the door
through which suffering enters
Tonight I am Jesus
Tomorrow I will be Judas

SARDINIA

The pebbled beach before the hotel
is dotted with German tourists and seaweed
Seasoned with the smiling Irish family
and topped with the beauty of the English girl
whose white body is remarkable
for her fifteen years

But my eyes can only caress the small breasts
of the little Italian girl who is selling postcards Unsuccessfully
The tight blue sweater

clings to the unprotected bosom
so round and soft
and climbs the peak of the hard little nipple
confident and glorious

I wish that I were that sweater
That I might drink that tiny brown figure
with my whole body
And be the envy of that tiny brown figure such as I

BEAUTY

I met a man I never knew
Of dark and mournful eye
And in his trembling hand he held
a golden butterfly
He stood before me, barred my path
Extended me his hand
"This beauty is too great" he said
"For me to understand"

I took the gift he offered me
as if it wasn't there
and looked upon the fragile life
Defenceless, in my care
Its wings were of some marvel silk
The colours rich and bright
But its body afraid and trembling
Its eyes as dark as night

I was bound to do my humane duty
and free it from my hand
For it knew not its own beauty
and could never understand
For beauty seems to be a magic which
dies when once aware
The beauty which makes this earth so rich
is now too close to despair

TIGER MOTH

Just before it touched town
the Tiger Moth danced briefly
in the sunset
Exalting in the freedom of
the last moment of its day
before its graceful silhouette
became one
with the old earth

Somewhere over by the hangar
its voice died
and the silence was disturbed only by
something in me which cried

with longing
for my body to rise
on De Havilland sails
To stretch upon a patchwork quilt
;this fragrant sunset of my imagination
Burrow in my cotton wool pillow
Roll over on my back to float in a sea of ecstasy
The Moth and I both smiling
on our cavortings
with ten thousand feet
of freedom
between us
and reality

But I am reality
and reality will always have its dreams

TIME MACHINE

In the course of their journey
Through the swirling mists of time
They were amazed to find
A place completely free
Of the corruption and squabbles of mankind

They all voted to stay, of course
And some of them had actually disembarked
When someone glanced at the Geiger counter
And noticing that the radiation level
Was dangerously high .
Recalled them

THE TIME OF MAN

The time of man will soon be here
When tongues fall silent with the smell of fear
When the shadow of death is drawing near
A relentless mighty flood
The manner of death is already planned
There's no escape from the master's hand
He has no need to sow the land
He'll stain it with our blood

Go, curse the dust from whence you came
You find you cannot name a name
No one on whom to lay the blame
The blame lies deep within
Sure we'd like to find some other place
But again we'd fertilize the race
With seeds of sorrow and disgrace
Mankind cannot change his skin
When we finally from its flesh are torn
Our earth will be a world reborn
Will flourish in a cleaner dawn
But we will never know

We lie upon our beds of nails
Speeding down those rusty rails
Still trying to hide our spiky tails
But there's nowhere else to go
And still we'll never think it fair
With the poisoned land, the toxic air
Corrupted nature everywhere

It would have happened anyway
There were a few who did despise
The smiling, helpful, warm disguise
Of those whose truths were merely lies
The bill is on its way

Can we look each other in the eye
As we contemplate this last goodbye
It's really not so hard to die
We've been practising on others
So take your neighbour by the hand
And kneel before the ravished land
Before we lay down in the sand
With our sisters and our brothers

THE HOLY WAR

"Where are you going?" he asked
"To the holy war" they replied

He laughed and said gaily
"Holy war, but there are no holy wars"

As one, they condemned him on the spot as a heathen
and he was run through by their many spears

Years later, one of their number recalled the incident
and reflected that, well, perhaps
he may have been right

The cause may have been holy
but the armies were evil

THE FRIDAY PRAYERS

The Friday prayers were finished
The young man dashed up to the muezzin
"your address was so thrilling
You are right, it is time to begin
Our next move must disclose our strength
No reason now to hide
I know that there are many who
will flock here to our side

"How come we haven't made contact before
Or are you just beginning?
Now I know that a man like you is with us
We're confident of winning"
The priest, smiling, spoke quietly
"How strangely you doth speak
Our next move is quite simple
We do the same next week"

I REMEMBER HIM

I remember him even today
The way he was
He had shrunk in old age
But his translucent skin had not
shrunk with him
Bagged and wrinkled
He had lived in his skin for many years
And it showed
The war was just meaningless history
To the new generation
To him and his comrades it had been
A universe in which they had abandoned
The best part of their lives

Or life itself

To be rewarded with a demob suit
In which to look for soulless work
on soul-destroying production lines
With just memories
To make the job endurable

I remember being shown pictures of him
As a young soldier in India
Laughing, fit, confident, muscular
About to dive off a thirty foot cliff
As if it was a doddle
He joined up in nineteen twenty seven

73

At the age of sixteen
And learned how to load horses and camels
And how to use a bayonet and
How to shoot to kill
And to co-exist with the rats in the trenches

And mourn for lost comrades
And survive
Also when the war was over
In a cold prefabricated three room hovel
Fit for a hero

He died in nineteen seventy seven
He was sixty six years old
I will never forget my father

UKRAINE I

So mankind reengages in one of its traditional activities
War
This time in Ukraine of all places
A country that nobody seems to have thought about too much
before now
Now the TV news channels are dominated
by explosions and scenes of burning buildings
Civilian apartment blocks
Not military targets
Women and children dossing down
in Underground stations

Before my TV conks out
Internet overloaded
By elderly german burghers sitting comfortably on sofas
chewing snacks
and thinking thank God it ain't us

It's a diversion from the humdrum
Beats third division football
and anyway Putin was generous enough
to hold off so we could watch
the olympics
Xi doubtless appreciated that

and anyway we did out bit
sent six thousand helmets to be used
by Ukranian citizens
as piss pots
If it becomes necessary

75

Ukraines President, Mr. Zelensky
Chooses to remain in Kiev, the capital
in spite of the bombardment and danger
of being captured
during a siege

        Good for him

He and Putin should fight it out
on the market place
in boxing gloves

Putin wouldn't stand a chance

But it would make great TV

UKRAINE II

They never knew they were going to war
till they were in it
Suddenly uniforms fighting back
Firing
And they suddenly realised, gape mouthed
 that it was live ammo
when one of the comrades folded over and fell
Bleeding
And died
The tyrant in his brooding bunker
Outwardly confident
of annihilating a nation

They'd not been bloody trained for this
War, real war
Not been bloody trained for anything really
The motivation of the enemy
vastly exceeding their own
Only wishing to go home
Far away from this strange
blood soaked place
and this logistics nightmare
of no grub
no juice for the trucks
no bloody ammo
freeze your arse off trying to sleep
and comrades with incomprehensible
dialects

77

The tyrant paces to and fro
Having expected the action to be over
within a couple of days
And now these bloody sanctions
Those incompetent idiotic generals
should have a taste of the old KGB
as he carefully composes himself
to tell lies on
TV

It's getting a bit desperate
We weren't prepared for this
and now were ordered to shoot anything
which moves
That should at least help us
to get home sooner
We don't need this fucking war
Those bastards fight like total fanatics
Hate the bastards You´d think they'd surrender instead of
fighting for this fucking dump

Hate this shit

It's cold

It's cold

It's cold

MEMORIES AND EPILOGUE

Memories can create an oppressive weight within the mind when you can find the time to think about them. I am at least happy that I still retain enough brain cells to allow me to ruffle through them occasionally, but trying to place them in some sort of order is getting to be next to impossible. It's no longer just a matter of remembering which year something took place, but even the decade. My ex wife is living in Brussels now, and although we created quite a few memories together in the few years we had, I've still no urge to go and visit her. To suffer my memories to be coloured by her vision of reality would be like tearing down a building housing a museum. A skyscraper really.

Through our estrangement I lost all contact to my daughter, and the years sailed by and she grew invisibly to womanhood before we could renew the relationship. You could not imagine the mental bombshell which hit me when our first meeting for over twenty years took place. I suppose I was half expecting the little girl I once knew to appear, but I was confronted with a fully mature and very attractive woman, and one, after hours of laughter and conversation, who appeared to share my ideas and ideals and was also, like me, a musician. I remember her mother wanted her to learn to be a secretary but her mentality is so similar to mine it would have been an office catastrophe. It's like an eerie mirror image of me in female. However, she doesn't drink. I can't imagine what happened there but at least we have one thing not in common.

It's somehow satisfying to have the knowledge that my genes made it into my daughter before her mothers did. Or there was a genetic battle which I won, and I still treasure memories of the baby girl who sat on my knee and got spoon fed occasionally and had no knowledge of profane language. She does now, but there again, so do I. It seems to be a result of the meagre vocabulary of most of the musicians I know that we all talk like that. Anyway, expression, language and the use of profanities have changed mightily over the past couple of generations, of which've survived three and a quarter.

The memories are still vivid but the lives have grown remote. I can't imagine what some of the people I knew years ago could be doing now. Ambitious we all were in different ways, though my ambitions have been softened by reality over the years. The more proficient I became in my chosen profession of musician and songwriter the more I aware that regardless of what you have to say and the way (in song) you've chosen to say it, only . about a tenth of the audience are really taking note of it. The rest are mostly listening to their inner voices telling them that the pubs close in two hours, and a pizza wouldn't be a bad idea - and what the heck is he singing about now?

I've not worn a suit and tie now for over forty years and I probably wouldn't be able to any more. I owned several and I seem to remember being treated a bit more respectfully by shop assistants while wearing one. I was very proud of my ability to tie a perfect windsor knot and could even tie a bow tie without outside help. Whatever happened to all those ties I got as Christmas presents? But living in jeans and tee shirts is much more practical. True, shop assistants ignore you more or less completely, but keep a beady eye open to see if you're stealing anything, but this is clothing you can even sleep in on park benches and suchlike, something I got used to on several tours of the USA. A jeans jacket is one of the most useful articles of clothing there is.

The inside pockets have capacity for loads of stuff, and even if you get soaked in some unavoidable downpour it'll just dry out and be as good as ever. The only people who wear suits these days are politicians and bank managers, both of whom with which I have somewhat strained relationships. I do know a lawyer who wears jeans under his robe. I suppose they all do these days.

The one constant in my life as long as I can remember is the guitar. I was given one as a kid, but being left-handed I had to change the strings around, rendering it permanently slightly out of tune, and anyway not knowing how to tune the thing I tuned it to what sounded nice, and that was an open chord. I played like that for a few years, even starting a band with my two brothers. Little did I know that I was tuning the instrument like the old bluesmen who were equally ignorant as to how it should be tuned.

When I finally discovered the correct tuning it meant learning all over again. Another problem was that I was always losing plectrums and was reduced to playing with my fingers. Painful at first but it proved extremely useful later on when playing harmonies on strings not adjacent to each other.

Another memory is of my dad bringing home a long playing record with the title "Down Home" by a guitarist named Chet Atkins. The guy played alone on the record, but at first I thought it was two or more guitarists until I twigged. That was it.
The hammer! It took me a few years without a teacher to conquer this new style, more or less, but it's served me in good stead throughout years of solo gigs. It sounds more like a ragtime piano than anything else, but you can adapt it to almost any kind of song. Then there are memories of musicians. Sessions. For example playing an open air as a duo with Chuck Leavell on a little stage which wouldn't stay still after a few drams. Touring through Switzerland with the Tannahill Weavers on a diet of Scotch whisky; playing a session in a pub in Bristol where my pal Al Johnson played the solo to beat all solos.

He was drunk at the time, which helped. Or trying to drink pint for pint with the immense Scottish folksinger Hamish Imlach which probably ended in disaster but is luckily not among my memories. Or performing solo at three thirty in the morning at a biker festival and getting a couple of thousand inebriated rockers to sing "you'll never walk alone"! These incidents are embedded permanently in the memory.

Then there is often the question of how did I come to poetry after writing songs for years. The answer is quite simple. Sitting in the band bus and just jotting ideas down for a potential new song, suddenly it turns into poetry. There's a subtle difference. Some songs are poems and some poems are songs. They are sometimes

intertwined. It's great on the stage to be able to read a song or sing a poem. It depends on how you, and the audience, feel.
Did I say earlier that memories are an oppressive weight? I take that back. They are like valuable companions to take along on life's journey - just like that song you'll never walk alone".
See you, maybe at the next concert.
Love, John

Printed in Poland
by Amazon Fulfillment
Poland Sp. z o.o., Wrocław
04 June 2022